OUR PLANET EARTH

Prairies

by Karen Latchana Kenney

BLASTOFF!
READERS
3

BELLWETHER MEDIA · MINNEAPOLIS, MN

Blastoff! Readers are carefully developed by literacy experts to build reading stamina and move students toward fluency by combining standards-based content with developmentally appropriate text.

Level 1 provides the most support through repetition of high-frequency words, light text, predictable sentence patterns, and strong visual support.

Level 2 offers early readers a bit more challenge through varied sentences, increased text load, and text-supportive special features.

Level 3 advances early-fluent readers toward fluency through increased text load, less reliance on photos, advancing concepts, longer sentences, and more complex special features.

★ **Blastoff! Universe**

Reading Level

Grade **K**

Grades **1–3**

Grade **4**

This edition first published in 2022 by Bellwether Media, Inc.

No part of this publication may be reproduced in whole or in part without written permission of the publisher. For information regarding permission, write to Bellwether Media, Inc., Attention: Permissions Department, 6012 Blue Circle Drive, Minnetonka, MN 55343.

Library of Congress Cataloging-in-Publication Data

Names: Kenney, Karen Latchana, author.
Title: Prairies / Karen Latchana Kenney.
Description: Minneapolis, MN : Bellwether Media, 2022. | Series: Blastoff! readers. Our planet Earth | Includes bibliographical references and index. | Audience: Ages 5-8 | Audience: Grades 2-3 |
Summary: "Simple text and full-color photography introduce beginning readers to prairies. Developed by literacy experts for students in kindergarten through third grade"-- Provided by publisher.
Identifiers: LCCN 2021011409 (print) | LCCN 2021011410 (ebook) | ISBN 9781644875230 (library binding) | ISBN 9781648344916 (paperback) | ISBN 9781648344312 (ebook)
Subjects: LCSH: Prairies--Juvenile literature.
Classification: LCC QH87.7 .K46 2022 (print) | LCC QH87.7 (ebook) | DDC 577.4/4--dc23
LC record available at https://lccn.loc.gov/2021011409
LC ebook record available at https://lccn.loc.gov/2021011410

Editor: Rebecca Sabelko   Designer: Jeffrey Kollock

Printed in the United States of America, North Mankato, MN.

Table of Contents

What Are Prairies?   4
Plants and Animals   12
People and Prairies   16
Glossary   22
To Learn More   23
Index   24

What Are Prairies?

Prairies are large grasslands. They are found in **temperate** areas around the world.

Prairies are mostly flat and treeless. They are sometimes called steppes or pampas.

Prairies form in the middle of **continents**. They receive just enough rain for grasses to grow well.

Prairie Grasses

Big Bluestem

- Tallgrass prairie grass
- up to 8 feet (2.4 meters) tall

Blue Grama

- Shortgrass prairie grass
- up to 2 feet (0.6 meters) tall

Tallgrass prairies receive the most rain. Shortgrass prairies are dry. Mixed prairies have tall and short grasses.

summer

winter

Prairie grasses must survive
harsh weather. Summers
are often hot and windy.
Winters are long and cold.

Adaptations help grasses survive. Hairy leaf surfaces protect against the sun and wind. Waxy leaves hold in water.

The Great Plains

Famous For

- Home to Plains Indian tribes for thousands of years

- Once home to 30 to 60 million bison

Size

- 1,125,000 square miles (2,913,737 square kilometers)

North America

 = Great Plains

Plants and Animals

great spangled
fritillary butterfly

Plants and animals help prairies **thrive**! Bees and butterflies **pollinate** wildflowers. Flowers' seeds feed hungry birds and prairie dogs.

Rabbits hide from coyotes in tall grasses. Prairie chickens peck for bugs.

coyote

Bison, wolves, and pronghorn used to be common in shortgrass prairies. Now their populations are small.

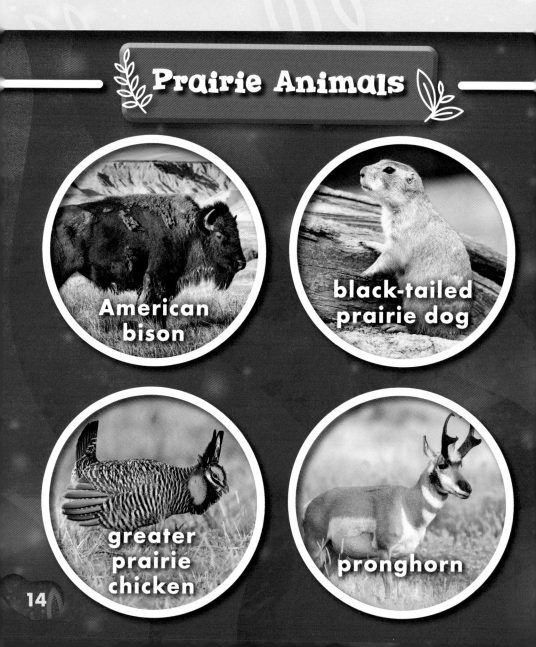

Prairie Animals

American bison

black-tailed prairie dog

greater prairie chicken

pronghorn

bunchgrass

prickly pear cactus

Today, cattle graze amongst **bunchgrasses** and prickly pear cacti.

oil pump

People use prairies in harmful ways. Some farming practices damage the soil.

Oil drilling harms animal habitats. **Invasive species** do, too. Animals cannot always adjust to changes.

How People Affect Prairies

- **Poor hunting habits harm animals**

- **Incorrect farming practices damage soil**

- **Invasive species harm habitats and animals**

19

People can help keep prairies
healthy. They can hunt responsibly.
They can be careful not to bring
harmful species into prairies.

Prairies are an important landform that must be **preserved**!

Glossary

adaptations—changes an animal or plant undergoes over a long period of time to fit where it lives

bunchgrasses—groups of grasses that mostly grow in the western United States

continents—the seven main land areas on Earth

disturbances—changes

diversity—the state of having many different forms or types

droughts—long periods of dry weather

grazing—feeding on plants on the ground

habitats—lands with certain types of plants, animals, and weather

invasive species—a species that is not originally from a region and causes harm to its new environment

nutrients—the things plants and animals need to grow

pollinate—to move pollen from one plant to another so that seeds will be made

preserved—kept from change

temperate—related to a mild climate that does not have extreme heat or cold

thrive—to grow well

To Learn More

AT THE LIBRARY

Boothroyd, Jennifer. *Let's Visit the Grassland.* Minneapolis, Minn.: Lerner Publications, 2017.

Doyle, Abby Badach. *20 Fun Facts about Grassland Habitats.* New York, N.Y.: Gareth Stevens Publishing, 2021.

Duling, Kaitlyn. *Prairie Dogs.* Minneapolis, Minn.: Bellwether Media, 2021.

ON THE WEB

FACTSURFER

Factsurfer.com gives you a safe, fun way to find more information.

1. Go to www.factsurfer.com.

2. Enter "prairies" into the search box and click Q.

3. Select your book cover to see a list of related content.

Index

adaptations, 9
animals, 12, 13, 14, 15, 16, 19, 20
continents, 6
droughts, 10
effects, 16, 18, 19
farming, 16, 17, 18
fires, 10
grass, 4, 6, 7, 8, 9, 13, 14, 15
grazing, 10, 11, 15, 16
Great Plains, 9
habitats, 16, 19
hunt, 16, 20
invasive species, 19, 20
Las Pampas, 10
location, 4, 6

nutrients, 11
oil drilling, 18, 19
pampas, 5
people, 16, 18, 19, 20
plants, 11, 12, 15, 16
protect, 9, 20, 21
rain, 6, 7
soil, 11, 16, 18
steppes, 5
summers, 8
water, 9
weather, 8
winters, 8